MATCH OF THE DAY MAG ANNUAL 2023

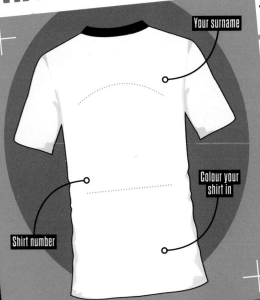

Your surname

Colour your shirt in

Shirt number

THIS BOOK BELONGS TO ....

AGE ....

MY FAVOURITE TEAM IS ....

MY FAVOURITE PLAYER IS ....

MY HIGHLIGHT OF 2022 WAS ....

WELCOME!

WOW! IT'S BEEN another incredible year of football — a rollercoaster of emotions filled with drama and excitement. This book celebrates the biggest stars and heroes in the game — so sit back and enjoy the read!

WHAT'S IN YOUR *MOTD MAG ANNUAL?*

ERLING HAALAND
P10 ALL HAIL HITMAN HAALAND!

P24 PREM PRIMARY'S SCHOOL TRIP!

P40 WORLD CUP PREVIEW!

WHO'S NOT INSIDE THIS BOOK...

PAUL THE PORTLY PIG

PRINCE CHARLES

SNOOKER LEGEND JOHN HIGGINS

TV STAR LORRAINE KELLY

THE BIG WINNERS OF 2022!

MAN. CITY PREMIER LEAGUE CHAMPIONS

City triumphed on the final day of the season after an epic title race with Liverpool — it was their fourth win in five seasons!

MOHAMED SALAH & SON HEUNG-MIN PREMIER LEAGUE GOLDEN BOOT

The Liverpool and Tottenham hitmen both bagged 23 goals — it was Salah's third Golden Boot win and Son's first!

LIVERPOOL FA CUP WINNERS

The Reds' dramatic penalty shootout win over Chelsea at Wembley was their first FA Cup victory for 16 years!

REAL MADRID UCL WINNERS

Carlo Ancelotti's men were crowned champions of Europe for a record 14th time after a 1-0 win over Liverpool in Paris!

CHELSEA WSL CHAMPIONS

Emma Hayes' all-conquering Chelsea team pipped Arsenal to top spot to claim their sixth WSL title and their third in a row!

96 PAGES *OF FOOTY FUN AND GAMES!*

THE £1.3 BILLION DREAM TEAM!

P50 BIG MONEY DREAM TEAM!

P77 THE ULTIMATE FOOTY QUIZ!

THE A-Z OF THE WORLD'S BEST WOMEN BALLERS!

P86 A-Z BEST WOMEN BALLERS!

5

MOTD MAG LOL! ZONE!

PEP GUARDIOLA

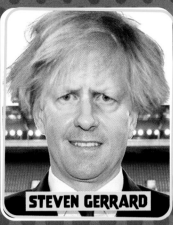

STEVEN GERRARD

4 BOSSES WITH BORIS' HAIR! →

BORIS JOHNSON OUT, THESE GUYS IN?

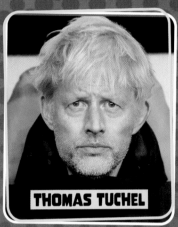

THOMAS TUCHEL

JURGEN KLOPP

4 FUNNY FACE SPLATS! ✔

CRAZY KEEPERS!

PLAYERS BURSTING FOR THE TOILET!

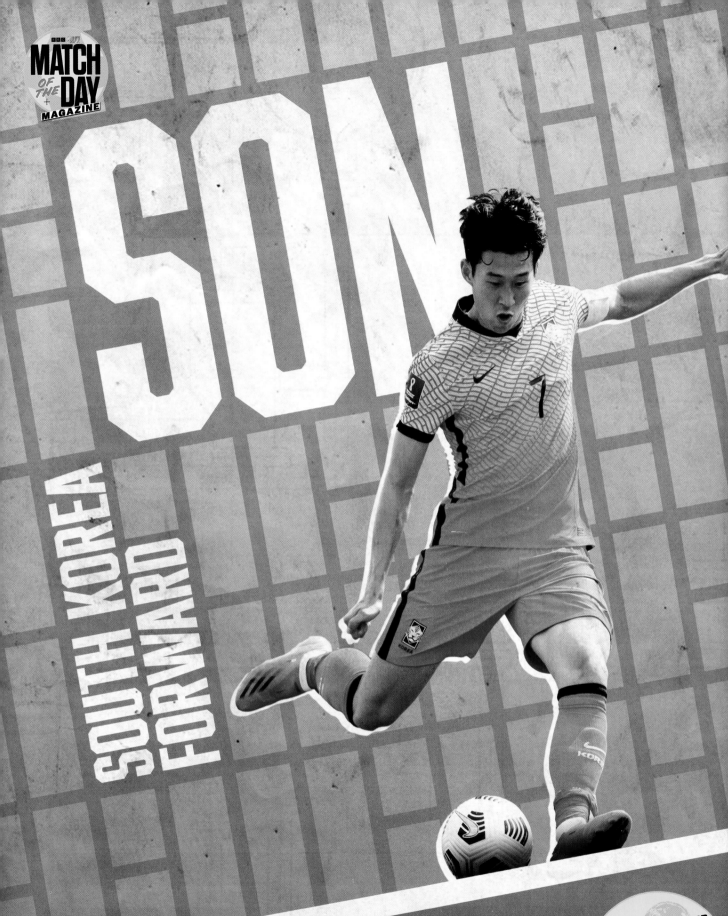

SON

SOUTH KOREA FORWARD

2022 WORLD CUP ICON!

THE CHAMPIONS QUIZ!

ANSWERS ON P92

Which club has won the MOST LEAGUE TITLES in each country below?

Ooh, good luck, human!

SPAIN

1

- A REAL MADRID
- B BARCELONA
- C ATLETICO MADRID

ITALY

SERIE A TIM

2

- A AC MILAN
- B INTER MILAN
- C JUVENTUS

TURKEY

SüperLig

3

- A FENERBAHCE
- B GALATASARAY
- C BESIKTAS

ENGLAND

4

- A LIVERPOOL
- B MAN. CITY
- C MAN. UNITED

SCOTLAND

SPFL
SCOTTISH PROFESSIONAL
FOOTBALL LEAGUE

5

- A ABERDEEN
- B CELTIC
- C RANGERS

GERMANY

6

- A BORUSSIA DORTMUND
- B BAYERN MUNICH
- C BAYER LEVERKUSEN

NETHERLANDS

7

- A AJAX
- B PSV EINDHOVEN
- C FEYENOORD

PORTUGAL

8

- A BENFICA
- B PORTO
- C SPORTING LISBON

WSL

9

- A ARSENAL
- B CHELSEA
- C MAN. CITY

YOUR FOOTY BRAIN POWER

9	GENIUS
7	PROFESSIONAL
5	SEMI-PRO
3	AMATEUR
1	SUNDAY LEAGUE
0	OH NO, DISASTER

YOUR SCORE ☐ /9

ERLING HA

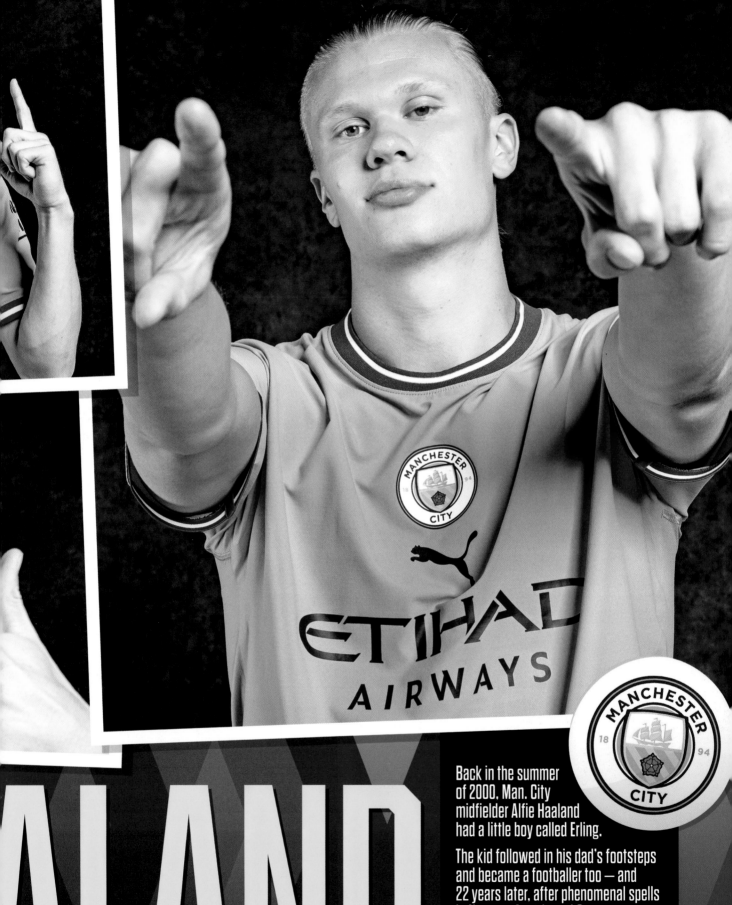

...ALAND

Back in the summer of 2000, Man. City midfielder Alfie Haaland had a little boy called Erling.

The kid followed in his dad's footsteps and became a footballer too — and 22 years later, after phenomenal spells in Norway, Austria and Germany, he is now also at Man. City.

This is the incredible tale of Erling Haaland — the 6ft 5in goal monster who has the world at his feet!

ERLING'S JOURNEY...

Erling's dad, Alfie Haaland!

THE STORY BEGINS IN JULY 2000 IN LEEDS, YORKSHIRE...

Norwegian midfielder Alfie Haaland, who's just left Leeds to sign for Man. City, is celebrating the birth of his baby boy. Little Erling is a three-year-old toddler when the family leaves England to move back to Bryne in Norway!

AT 15 HE'S PLAYING IN NORWAY'S TOP DIVISION...

Erling works his way up through Bryne's academy and makes his debut in the Norwegian top-flight three months before his 16th birthday. He soon catches the eye of future Man. United boss Ole Gunnar Solskjaer, who signs him for Molde in 2017!

THE HAALAND HYPE IS REAL...

In his second season with Molde, at the age of 18, he nets 16 goals in 30 games, finishing as the club's top scorer. Word of his insane goal-scoring talent spreads across Europe with a host of top clubs keen to sign him!

A SUPERSTAR STRIKER IS BORN...

Despite interest from the continent's biggest clubs, Haaland decides to join Austrian champions RB Salzburg — and it's here his goalscoring superpowers really shine. In his first, and only full season with Salzburg, he smashes 28 goals in just 22 games!

HAALAND HEADS TO GERMANY...

Man. United and Juventus are reportedly scrapping it out for Haaland's signature when he makes a surprise £20m switch to German club Borussia Dortmund. It's in Germany, over the next two-and-a-half seasons, that he makes his name as the planet's most fearsome young striker!

NOBODY CAN STOP THE DORTMUND DESTROYER...

Haaland rewrites the Dortmund history books, becoming an instant legend. In just 89 games for the BVB he scores a staggering 86 goals, wins Bundesliga Player of the Year and top scores in the Champions League. Now, he's on the shopping list of every club in the world!

IN HIS FATHER'S FOOTSTEPS...

In June 2022, after months of speculation and a gazillion goals, Haaland puts pen to paper on a five-year contract at the Etihad after City stumped up the £51m release clause. Erling's fantastic football journey continues at the club his dad played for 22 years earlier!

HITMAN HAALAND!

The incredible numbers behind the Norwegian assassin!

FACTFILE!

Full name	Erling Braut Haaland
Date of birth	21 July 2000 (age 21)
Place of birth	Leeds, England
Height	6ft 4in
Position	Striker
Preferred foot	Left

HAALAND'S LAST 3 SEASONS!

SEASON	GAMES	GOALS
2019-20	40	44
2020-21	41	41
2021-22	30	29

5 HAALAND HIGHLIGHTS!

1 In 2020, Haaland won the Golden Boy award for being the world's best player under the age of 21!

2 In 2021, he was named Bundesliga Player of the Season and included in the FIFA FIFPro World 11!

3 Haaland has the best minutes-per-goal ratio in the history of the Bundesliga — he averaged a goal every 87 minutes for Borussia Dortmund!

4 He also has the best minutes-per-goal ratio in Champions League history, scoring on average every 64 minutes!

5 Erling is the only player ever to score 20 Champions League goals before the age of 21 – it only took him 14 games!

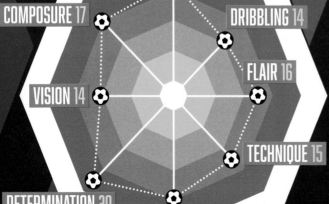

ERLING'S GOAL STATS!

MOLDE 2017-18

GAMES	GOALS	GOALS PER GAME
50	20	0.4

RB SALZBURG 2018-20

GAMES	GOALS	GOALS PER GAME
27	29	1.07

BORUSSIA DORTMUND 2020-22

GAMES	GOALS	GOALS PER GAME
89	86	0.97

NORWAY 2019-

GAMES	GOALS	GOALS PER GAME
21	20	0.95

ERLING HAALAND'S TEKKERS WHEEL!

His ratings out of 20 on Football Manager 2022!

- FINISHING 18
- DRIBBLING 14
- COMPOSURE 17
- FLAIR 16
- VISION 14
- TECHNIQUE 15
- DETERMINATION 20
- PACE 19

WHAT'S ON

Anyone seen the remote?

NOT COMING TO YOUR SCREENS ANY TIME SOON!

FRIDAY

SEAMUS COALMAN

7am CBBC ■ The feisty Irish coalminer discovers the true meaning of fear when he bumps into a familiar face down at the local depot.

HUNTING FOR NESSIE WITH LIONEL MESSI

★★★★★★★★★☆☆

11am BBC One ■ Lionel's obsessive one-man search for the Loch Ness Monster takes a sinister twist when a local butcher attempts to muscle in on the hunt.

THE LION KING

3pm BBC Two ■ Last in series. Chester Zoo security team embarks on a dramatic rescue mission as Josh King's attempt to crawl through the zoo's lion enclosure ends in disaster. Contains upsetting scenes.

EEJIT McDAFTY

9pm BBC One ■ New series. Aston Villa midfielder John McGinn is back as Scotland's much-loved, bungling detective Eejit McDafty.

COSTA, DEL, SOL: FUN IN THE SUN

11pm BBC Three ■ It's week two of Diego Costa, Dele Alli and Sol Campbell's self-catering holiday in Fuengirola. Tenison rises after Diego spills bin juice over Sol's linen slacks.

TV IN 2023?

SATURDAY

BAMBOOZLE THAT POODLE
7am CBBC ■ Roy Hodgson hosts another episode of his chaotic award-winning wibbly-wobbly gameshow, with Mark Noble, Phillip Schofield and a dozen miniature poodles.

KYLIAN'S KOALA KARAOKE
9am BBC Two ■ Footy megastar Kylian Mbappe is back Down Under with a brand-new series of his marsupial talent show. Can reigning koala champion Kevin defend his title?

FRED IN HIS SHED
5pm BBC Two ■ Man. United's Brazilian Fred hosts his weekly DIY show live from his Salford shed. Today he's unblocking a toilet with a Gregg's sausage roll and a balloon.

HARRY MAGUIRE FIGHTING FIRE
9.30pm BBC Two
■ In this gritty northern drama, the big England centre-back plays a lonely simpleton who's lost his job, dog and all hope — but the opening of a new fire station changes his life.

BENTEKE FRIED CHICKEN
10pm BBC Four
Belgian striker Christian Benteke is back with his award-winning, laugh-a-minute cookery show. Will retired ref Mike Dean survive Benteke's infamous batter challenge?

SUNDAY

FIREMAN SAM
7am CBeebies ■ Last in series. After four weeks of intensive training at Preston Fire Station an excited Sam Johnstone finally gets to drive the station's fire engine. But disaster lurks around the very first corner.

BEN & LOLLEY'S LITTLE KINGDOM
★★★★★★★★★★★
8am CBeebies ■ In amongst the thorny brambles, it's the cartoon capers of twinkle-toed winger Joe Lolley and Chile striker Ben Brereton Diaz. How will they deal with Gaston's shock revelation?

FILM

ALISSON WONDERLAND
1.30pm BBC One ■ Classic family fun. The Liverpool keeper falls down a rabbit hole and lands into a fantasy world full of weird, wonderful people and animals.

CHICKEN TIKKA MO SALAH
4.30pm BBC One ■ Hazel Irvine joins Mo in Mumbai for some Indian cooking, sunset paddleboarding, cricket lessons and a midnight hunt for some city-dwelling leopards.

OBI-WAN IWOBI
9pm BBC Two ■ Fly-on-the-wall documentary following Star Wars superfan Alex Iwobi. This week Alex is left distraught when the 100% genuine real-life Ewok he bought off eBay turns out to be not as it seems.

17

2022 WORLD CUP ICON!

MESSI

ARGENTINA / FORWARD

WIN!

THE ULTIMATE KIDS FOOTY PRIZE!

- 55-INCH TV 4K SMART TV
- FOLDING FOOTBALL GAME TABLE
- 2 x LIGHT-UP INDOOR FOOTBALLS
- 2 x PERSONALISABLE MINI FOOTBALLS WITH COLOURING PENS
- £100 TAKEAWAY VOUCHER OF THE WINNER'S CHOICE
- ONE YEAR MATCH OF THE DAY MAGAZINE SUBSCRIPTION

WOW! One lucky Match of the Day magazine Annual reader is going to win the most amazing footy bundle EVER! To be in with a chance of winning more than £1,000 of goodies, just answer the question below!

EPIC TABLE FOOTBALL!

MOTD MAG SUBSCRIPTION!

SICK 55-INCH TV!

Q Which Tottenham player shared the 2021-22 Premier League Golden Boot with Liverpool's Mohamed Salah?

A Harry Kane
B Son Heung-Min
C Lucas Moura

HOW TO ENTER

BY EMAIL Send to 14963@motdcomps.co.uk and put the code 14963 in the email subject line. Don't forget to include your answer, name and contact number.

BY TEXT Text COMP [space] then MOTD14963+ either A, B or C [space] plus your name and contact number to 66644. Text entry cost will be however much your mobile phone company charges for one standard text at time of entry. **CLOSING DATE** 11.59pm, 31 March 2023

You can enter if you are over 18 and live in England, Wales, Scotland, Northern Ireland or the Channel Islands. Promoter: Ebury, The Random House Group Ltd. Competition administered by Immediate Media Company London Ltd. See opposite & p83 for full T&Cs.

DO YOU REMEMBER THE 2021-22 TITLE RACE?

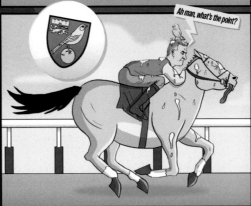

These angry birds are no soft touch!

Currently having ANOTHER overhaul!

Gold all day for the megabucks Toon!

UCL Spurs are off on their travels!

It's all about Mbappe at PSG!

20

PICTURES!

HOW TO BE A STAR!

Here's what you need to be like your baller hero!

HAALAND STARTER KIT

TERMINATOR GOAL VISION!

A DAD WHO PLAYED FOR MAN. CITY!

AN INSATIABLE HUNGER FOR GOALS!

BOOTS WORN OUT FROM SCORING GOALS!

MESSI STARTER KIT

YOUR FAVOURITE PYJAMA TOP!

BALLON D'OR COLLECTION TO CHEER YOU UP WHEN LIVING IN A NEW CITY!

A LOVE FOR ARGENTINA!

FRENCH BOOK FOR ESSENTIAL PHRASES!

WHAT WILL WE SEE IN 2023?

Do YOU think these things will happen next year?

Declan Rice named England captain

YES ☑ **NO** ☑

A three-way title playoff in the WSL

YES ☑ **NO** ☑

Man. City winning the Champions League

YES ☑ **NO** ☑

Liverpool winning the Premier League

YES ☑ **NO** ☑

TOP 10
WSL GOAL MACHINES!

We count down the ten players who've scored the MOST WSL GOALS since it kicked off in 2011!

MORE THAN 500 GOALS BETWEEN THEM!

10

42 goals
147 games
FARA WILLIAMS
Retired
Age: 38 Country: England

9
42 goals
46 games
SAM KERR
Chelsea
Age: 28 Country: Australia

8

50 goals
148 games
JORDAN NOBBS
Arsenal
Age: 29 Country: England

7

50 goals
127 games
NIKITA PARRIS
Arsenal
Age: 28 Country: England

6

50 goals
113 games
KIM LITTLE
Arsenal
Age: 32 Country: Scotland

5

52 goals
128 games
BETH MEAD
Arsenal
Age: 27 Country: England

22

4

54 goals
85 games

FRAN KIRBY
Chelsea
Age: 29 Country: England

3

55 goals
127 games

BETH ENGLAND
Chelsea
Age: 28 Country: England

1

VISIT RWANDA

74 goals
89 games

VIVIANNE MIEDEMA
Arsenal
Age: 25 Country: Netherlands

2

61 goals
142 games

ELLEN WHITE
Man. City
Age: 33 Country: England

Welcome to
Premier League Primary School

No pets * No fighting * No eggs

25

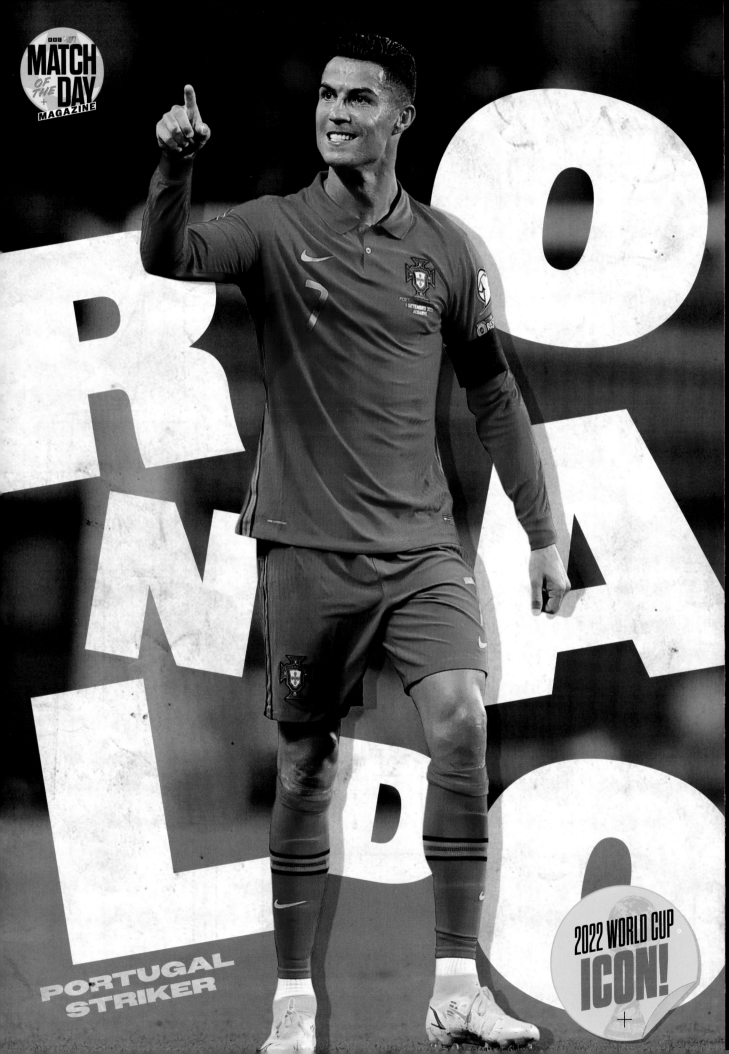

MATCH OF THE DAY MAGAZINE

RONALDO

PORTUGAL STRIKER

2022 WORLD CUP ICON!

23 THINGS TO DO IN 2023!

Your mission is to COMPLETE ALL OF THESE CHALLENGES starting in January 2023. Good luck!

ON THE PITCH...

2 LOB THE KEEPER FROM OUTSIDE THE AREA!

THE SIGHT OF a keeper frantically back-pedalling before falling over and flapping at thin air is a wonderful one for any attacker. A perfectly weighted lob is a beautiful thing to witness!

MISSION COMPLETED

1 SCORE A PERFECT + HAT-TRICK!

BAGGING THREE GOALS in a game will instantly make you a hero — but can you complete the ultimate hatty challenge of a goal with your right foot, one with your left foot and one with your head?

MISSION COMPLETED

3 DO MORE THAN 100 KEEPY-UPPIES!

THERE'S ONLY ONE way to master this — practice, practice, and more practice. Don't kick it too hard, keep on your toes and use any part of your body — feet, thighs, head and shoulders!

MISSION COMPLETED

4 MAKE UP A CELEBRATION WITH YOUR MATES AND BUST IT OUT IN A MATCH!

FOOTBALL SHOULD BE fun. Football should be a laugh. So why not spend some time with your team-mates working on a lol goal cele in training so you can perform it when you score in a real game!

MISSION COMPLETED

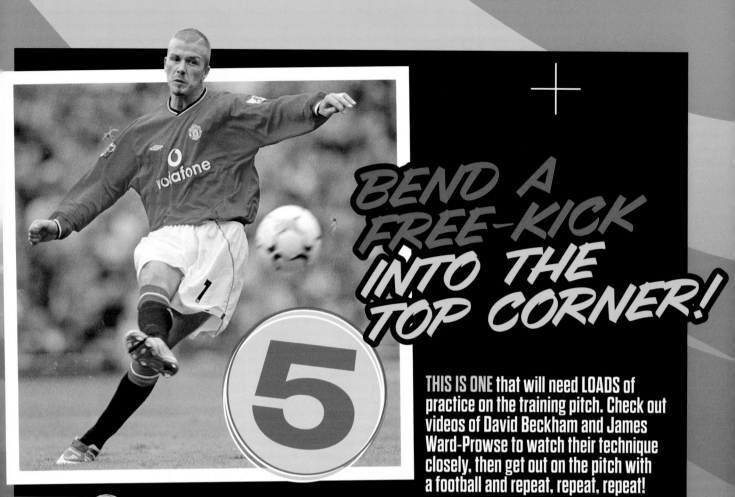

BEND A FREE-KICK INTO THE TOP CORNER!

5

THIS IS ONE that will need **LOADS** of practice on the training pitch. Check out videos of David Beckham and James Ward-Prowse to watch their technique closely, then get out on the pitch with a football and repeat, repeat, repeat!

MISSION COMPLETED ✔

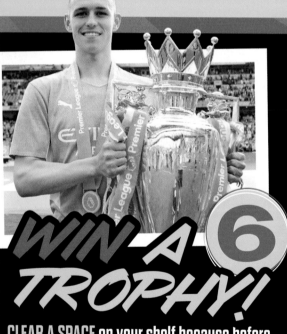

WIN A TROPHY!

6

CLEAR A SPACE on your shelf because before the year ends there will be a shiny cup on there. It doesn't matter what it is — a league title, a cup win, a Player of the Year award or one for most-improved player, put 100% in on the training pitch and you **WILL** be rewarded!

MISSION COMPLETED ✔

PERFECT THE CRUYFF TURN AND USE IT IN A GAME!

7

INVENTED BY THE legendary Dutch baller Johann Cruyff in 1974 and still one of the sickest pieces of skill you can bust out. But it's not easy — so put in the hours on the training ground first!

MISSION COMPLETED ✔

ON THE PITCH...

SMASH AN UNSTOPPABLE VOLLEY OFF THE UNDERSIDE OF THE BAR! 9

THE NOISE OF the ball smacking the bottom of the crossbar and then bouncing up into the roof of the net is probably the greatest sound known to man — and it looks sick, too!

MISSION COMPLETED

BEAT THE KEEPER 8 WITH AN OVERHEAD KICK!

ANOTHER THING THAT requires serious practice. Get a mate to cross the ball to you, over and over again. Expect to miss the ball, expect to shin it and expect to get muddy — but it'll totally be worth it!

MISSION COMPLETED

DINK A PANENKA! 10

TO PULL OFF this ultimate bit of tekkers — the king of pens — you need nerves of steel and supreme confidence. Stride up to the ball as if you're going to blast it, but instead, cheekily chip it down the middle as the keeper dives to the side!

MISSION COMPLETED

SCORE A DIVING HEADER!

ONE OF THE most underrated types of goal in the game. Very few things in life can match the beauty of a player, fully horizontal, flying through the air and powering a header past a stunned keeper!

MISSION COMPLETED

+12 MAKE A REMARKABLE GOAL-LINE CLEARANCE!

STRIKERS GET ALL the glory but we're here for the hero defenders too. Whether it's a reflex header, a brave block or a full-stretch hook off the line, a dramatic clearance is as good as a goal!

MISSION COMPLETED ✓

13 SAVE A PENALTY!

A PENALTY STOP is the moment that keepers can become legends too. Make yourself look as big as possible and stare into the eyes of the penalty taker. A match-winning spot-kick save in a shootout can see you write your name into your team's history books!

MISSION COMPLETED ✓

14 GIVE A MOTIVATIONAL TEAM-TALK TO INSPIRE A SECOND-HALF COMEBACK!

YOU'VE TRUDGED BACK into the dressing room at half-time with your team 2-0 down. Heads are down, but this is your chance to shine. Remind your team-mates how good they are, and tell them they can go out there and turn it around!

MISSION COMPLETED ✓

GO TO THE FA CUP FINAL AT WEMBLEY! 15

THE WALK UP Wembley Way, the sea of colourful flags and scarves, the incredible cup final atmosphere and being able to tell your mates at school you were there — YOU were at the FA Cup final. Priceless!

MISSION COMPLETED ✓

WATCH A MATCH IN EVERY DIVISION IN ENGLAND! 16

THERE'S LIFE OUTSIDE the Prem. It might not be as glam as the top flight but the Football League, from Accrington Stanley to Wycombe, oozes tradition and every ground gives you a different experience!

MISSION COMPLETED ✓

GO TO A LOCAL DERBY FOR A NIGHT MATCH! 17

THE BUTTERFLIES IN your stomach, the dream of a last-minute winner and the agony of defeat — derbies are nerve-wracking affairs. And under the glow of floodlights, the atmosphere is always incredible!

MISSION COMPLETED ✓

18 WATCH LIONEL MESSI LIVE!

THE GREATEST OF All Time is now 35 — so sometime soon those magic feet of his are going to stop performing miracles. You may not get many more chances to see legendary Leo in the flesh!

MISSION COMPLETED ✓

19 TRAVEL TO AN AWAY GAME!

THERE'S SOMETHING SPECIAL about following your team away from home — whether it's in the car with your scarf fluttering out of the window, on the train counting down the stops or singing away on the supporters' coach. Win, lose or draw, it's all about a great day out!

MISSION COMPLETED ✓

+20
TAKE A SELFIE WITH A PREM FOOTBALLER!

YOU'RE NOT LIKELY to bump into a footy star in your local Morrison's or walking the dog — but always be prepared and have a phone handy. On holiday in the summer, around a club's training ground or at a stadium on match day are the most likely spots!

MISSION COMPLETED ✓

BUY A RANDOM FOREIGN FOOTY SHIRT AND SUPPORT THEM! 21

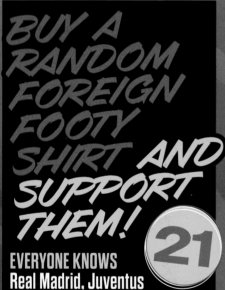

EVERYONE KNOWS Real Madrid, Juventus and PSG — time to mix it up a bit. Some of the coolest kits out there belong to lesser-known teams — so stand out from the crowd with a new shirt — and a new foreign team to support!

MISSION COMPLETED ✓

VISIT AN ICONIC EUROPEAN STADIUM! 22

MAINLAND EUROPE IS littered with legendary football stadiums — you've just got to find them. If you're travelling abroad with your parents, plan in a trip to the city or region's biggest stadium — it's a fun way to spend a couple of hours!

MISSION COMPLETED ✓

GET YOURSELF TO A WSL MATCH! 23

THE WOMEN'S GAME has never been so popular, and after the Euros the crowds are getting bigger and bigger. So get yourself along to see some of the best female ballers out there doing their thing!

MISSION COMPLETED ✓

BRAZIL 10 FORWARD

2022 WORLD CUP
ICON!

NEYMAR

WOULD YOU RATHER...?

Grab a mate and tackle these SIX HUGE footballing dilemmas!

 **OR**

WIN THE PREMIER LEAGUE WITH THE TEAM YOU SUPPORT

SCORE THE GOAL TO WIN YOUR COUNTRY THE WORLD CUP

 **OR**

BE BEST MATES WITH WEST HAM BOSS DAVID MOYES

BE BEST MATES WITH ADAM LA LLAMA

 **OR**

SIGN FOR REAL MADRID AND GET THE No.7 SHIRT

SIGN FOR BARCELONA AND GET THE No.10 SHIRT

 **OR**

WEAR KEEPER GLOVES EVERY DAY FOR A YEAR

WEAR A REFEREE'S KIT EVERY DAY FOR A YEAR

 **OR**

YOUR TEAM HAD KYLIAN MBAPPE ON LOAN FOR TWO MONTHS

YOUR TEAM HAD NEYMAR FOR THE WHOLE SEASON

 **OR**

WIN THE PREMIER LEAGUE GOLDEN BOOT

BE NAMED PFA PLAYER OF THE YEAR

35

IT'S TIME TO RANK YOUR RICE!

Here's some **FOOD FOR THOUGHT**, readers!

1 JASMINE RICE

MY RATING! ☐/10

2 RICE PUDDING

MY RATING! ☐/10

3 BASMATI RICE

MY RATING! ☐/10

4 EGG FRIED RICE

MY RATING! ☐/10

5 BLACK RICE

MY RATING! ☐/10

6 RISOTTO RICE

MY RATING! ☐/10

7 DECLAN RICE

MY RATING! ☐/10

8 STICKY RICE

MY RATING! ☐/10

Goodness of a Simple Grain
Kellogg's
RICE KRISPIES

9 RICE KRISPIES

MY RATING! ☐/10

MY TOP 3 RICES!

1 ....

2 ....

3 ....

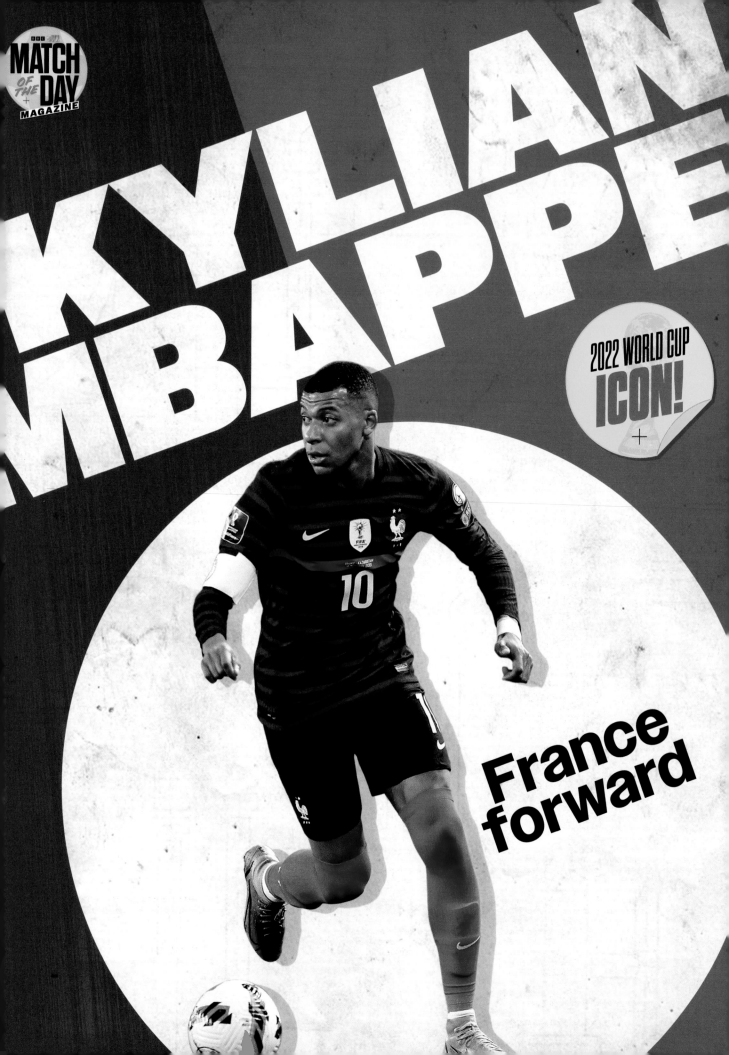

YOUR BIG WINNERS OF 2023!

Our wicked word grids below will help you PREDICT NEXT YEAR'S HEROES!

GRID 1
THE FIRST CLUB NAME YOU SEE IS YOUR 2022-23 PREMIER LEAGUE TITLE WINNER!

```
S B N A S S W B W L
M S P U R S E R O I
A T A D C R S I L V
N E R U H N T G V E
C R S N E A H H E R
I L E K L N A T S P
T I N R S D M O N O
Y N A C E E S N E O
F U L H A M U S O L
S M A N U N I T E D
```

GRID 2
THE FIRST CLUB NAME YOU SEE IS YOUR 2022-23 CHAMPIONS LEAGUE WINNER!

```
S I N B L F X M D R
A N B A I E T P E E
C T A R V R G O B A
M E C C E N N R M L
I R H E R A C T A M
L A E L P S G O N A
A J L O O D R K C D
N A S N O E S A I R
H X E A L S U S T I
S B A Y E R N R Y D
```

GRID 3
THE FIRST SURNAME YOU SEE IS YOUR 2022-23 PREM GOLDEN BOOT WINNER!

```
S C N A S F X M D S
G S B F C E T O E K
R N U N E Z J O T A
H A A L A N D X H N
S A K A P A C S A E
L L O S O N O A V Q
V A R D Y D L N E M
M I T R O V I C R A
H G W O O D S H T N
S A L A H F E O Z I
```

GRID 4
THE FIRST SURNAME YOU SEE IS YOUR 2022-23 PFA PLAYER OF THE YEAR WINNER!

```
S C N A S F X M D A
G S B F C E T O M A
O D E G A A R D O N
E Z E U D I A Z U E
A D I A S A K A N E
M A G U I R E A T S
T H I A G O R K S A
D E B R U Y N E O L
H G W X F O D E N A
S R I C E F R E D H
```

MY WINNERS OF 2023

PREMIER LEAGUE _____   CHAMPIONS LEAGUE _____
GOLDEN BOOT _____   PLAYER OF THE YEAR _____

KANE

ENGLAND
STRIKER

2022 WORLD CUP
ICON!

ULTIMATE GUIDE TO THE

2022 WORLD CUP!

Four years ago in Russia, Kylian Mbappe and France celebrated winning the World Cup. This winter in the Middle East they will defend their trophy!

Could be a bumpy ride!

QATAR 2022!

1 THE BIG KICK-OFF!

Stick it in your diary — Monday 21 November 2022 — that's when the 22nd World Cup kicks off with Senegal v Netherlands!

2 ROAD TO GLORY!

Thirty-two teams will battle it out over 28 days to be crowned champions of the world — this will be the last World Cup with 32 teams, as it's increasing to 48 for the 2026 tournament!

3 EYES ON THE PRIZE!

Record five-time winners Brazil are looking for their sixth title, 2018 winners France will be keen to defend their trophy — and England's recent tournament record means they will be feared!

4 UNFAMILIAR FACES!

Host nation Qatar are making their World Cup debut, Canada have qualified for their first tournament since 1986 and Gareth Bale's Wales are making their first World Cup appearance for 64 years!

5 MISSING OUT!

Euro 2020 winners Italy failed to qualify for their second successive World Cup, Mohamed Salah's Egypt will also not be taking part in Qatar, and neither will Scotland or Northern Ireland!

6 THE STAGE IS SET!

Eight futuristic stadiums will host a total of 64 matches — the biggest of which is the 80,000-capacity Lusail Iconic Stadium, which will stage the final on Sunday 18 December!

7 MAD MASCOT!

This isn't a ghost — it's La'eeb, the mascot of the 2022 World Cup. La'eeb is an Arabic word meaning 'super-skilled player' and he comes from a parallel world where tournament mascots live!

8 SICK BALL!

The official match ball, made by Adidas, is called Al Rihla, which means 'The Journey' in Arabic. They say it was inspired by the culture, architecture, iconic boats and the flag of Qatar!

9 GEOGRAPHY LESSON!

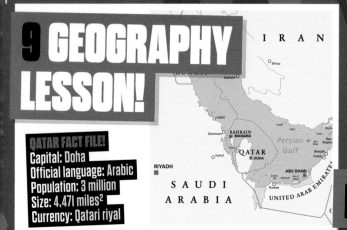

QATAR FACT FILE!
Capital: Doha
Official language: Arabic
Population: 3 million
Size: 4,471 miles²
Currency: Qatari riyal

Qatar is a country in the Middle East, and one of the richest in the world, thanks to its oil. Most of the country consists of desert and it gets seriously hot in the summer!

10 AWESOME ANIMALS!

The national animal of Qatar is the Arabian oryx, but you will also find ostriches, lizards, jackals and honey badgers. Qatar's biggest mammal is actually a dugong, also known as a sea cow!

WHO IS GOING TO WIN IT?

BRAZIL

DEFENSIVE DESTROYERS AND FIRE FORWARDS!

Manager: Tite
Captain: Rotating
Nickname: A Selecao
World Cup best: Winners (1958, 1962, 1970, 1994, 2002)
2018 World Cup: Quarter-finals (Brazil 1-2 Belgium)
Last trophy: Copa America (2019)

STAR MEN

Neymar

Vinicius Junior

Alisson Becker

They've won this tournament more than any other country — but not for 20 years. They cruised through qualifying, remaining unbeaten, and if Neymar is fit and in the mood, it spells danger to every other team!

ENGLAND

PATIENT PASSING WITH A LETHAL STRIKER!

Manager: Gareth Southgate
Captain: Harry Kane
Nickname: The Three Lions
World Cup best: Winners (1966)
2018 World Cup: Semi-finals (England 1-2 Croatia)
Last trophy: World Cup (1966)

STAR MEN

Harry Kane

Phil Foden

Declan Rice

It may be 56 years since England lifted a trophy but a run to the semis at the last World Cup and reaching the final of Euro 2020 has given the Three Lions reasons to believe — could it be third time lucky for Gareth Southgate?

FRANCE

BIG EGOS, BIG NAMES AND BIG TALENTS!

Manager: Didier Deschamps
Captain: Hugo Lloris
Nickname: Les Bleus
World Cup best: Winners (1998, 2018)
2018 World Cup: Winners
Last trophy: UEFA Nations League (2021)

STAR MEN

Kylian Mbappe

N'Golo Kante

Karim Benzema

A superstar squad packed with elite talent and supreme confidence, the 2018 World Cup winners are favourites to retain their trophy. With Kylian Mbappe and Karim Benzema in attack, who can stop them?

ARGENTINA

LIONEL MESSI & TEN OTHERS!

Manager: Lionel Scaloni
Captain: Lionel Messi
Nickname: La Albiceleste
World Cup best: Winners (1978, 1986)
2018 World Cup: Round of 16 (Argentina 3-4 France)
Last trophy: Copa America (2021)

STAR MEN

Lionel Messi

Lautaro Martinez

Rodrigo de Paul

Like Brazil, Argentina sailed unbeaten through South American qualifying. This will surely be Lionel Messi's final World Cup — and it's the only trophy he's never won. Can he fire his country to their first win since 1986?

SPAIN

CLASSIC PASS-AND-MOVE BALLERS!

Manager: Luis Enrique
Captain: Sergio Busquets
Nickname: La Roja
World Cup best: Winners (2010)
2018 World Cup: Round of 16 (Spain 1-1 Russia) (lost on penalties)
Last trophy: Euros (2012)

STAR MEN

Rodri

Ansu Fati

Pedri

The all-conquering Spanish team of 2008-2012 is long gone and this is a fresh squad with new names and new faces — but a run to the semis at Euro 2020 showed they could be about to produce something special again!

BELGIUM

SUPERSTAR ATTACKERS & FREE FLOWING FOOTY!

Manager: Roberto Martinez
Captain: Eden Hazard
Nickname: De Rode Duivels
World Cup best: Third Place (2018)
2018 World Cup: Semi-finals (Belgium 0-1 France)
Last trophy: n/a

STAR MEN

Kevin De Bruyne

Romelu Lukaku

Thibaut Courtois

Any team with Kevin De Bruyne, a fully fit Eden Hazard and an in-form Romelu Lukaku can destroy whatever is in front of them. But this could be the last chance of glory for Belgium's famous golden generation!

THE RACE FOR THE GOLDEN BOOT!

THE 2018 GOLDEN BOOT WINNER

HARRY KANE
ENGLAND

Club: Tottenham **Age:** 29

73 | 50
ENGLAND GAMES | ENGLAND GOALS

World Cup games/goals: 6/6

Harry was the top scorer at the last World Cup but he'll be smashing a huge record if he does it again in Qatar. No player in the history of football has ever won the World Cup Golden Boot twice!

THE ALL-TIME TOP SCORER

CRISTIANO RONALDO
PORTUGAL

Club: Man. United **Age:** 37

189 | 117
PORTUGAL GAMES | PORTUGAL GOALS

World Cup games/goals: 17/7

International football's record scorer shows no signs of slowing down — he's netted 32 times in his last 35 games. CR7 has won every Golden Boot at club and international level, except this one!

THE GREATEST OF ALL TIME

LIONEL MESSI
ARGENTINA

Club: PSG **Age:** 35

162 | 86
ARGENTINA GAMES | **ARGENTINA GOALS**

World Cup games/goals: 19/6

Just like his nemesis CR7, Leo has one final shot at World Cup glory in Qatar. He fired his country to glory at last year's Copa America in 2021, can he add the big one to his amazing collection of medals?

THE ELITE-LEVEL ENTERTAINER

NEYMAR
BRAZIL

Club: PSG **Age:** 30

119 | 74
BRAZIL GAMES | **BRAZIL GOALS**

World Cup games/goals: 10/6

He's a megastar in his homeland, but a stop-start time at PSG has seen the doubters pile on. Can he shut them up by becoming the first Brazilian winner since Ronaldo 20 years ago?

THE WORLD'S TOP TALENT

KYLIAN MBAPPE
FRANCE

Club: PSG **Age:** 23

57 | 27
FRANCE GAMES | **FRANCE GOALS**

World Cup games/goals: 7/4

Football agrees that Kylian is a 100% GOAT of the future. His electric pace and finishing is already the stuff of legend — and 150 goals in his last 173 games for PSG shows he can score for fun!

THE EXPERT BIG-GAME FINISHER!

KARIM BENZEMA
FRANCE

Club: Real Madrid **Age:** 34

97 | 37
FRANCE GAMES | **FRANCE GOALS**

World Cup games/goals: 5/3

He's more than ten years older than his French strike partner — but Benzy has been equally unstoppable at club level over the past four seasons, scoring 131 goals for Real in that time!

2021-22

BAYERN MUNICH
BUNDESLIGA CHAMPIONS

AC MILAN
SERIE A
CHAMPIONS

LE
WIN

LEAGUE WINNERS

REAL MADRID
LA LIGA CHAMPIONS

CAMPEONES

TEMPORADA 2021/2022

PSG
LIGUE 1 CHAMPIONS

LIGUE 1 Uber Eats
CHAMPION 2022

CELTIC
SCOTTISH PREMIERSHIP CHAMPIONS

CHELSEA
WSL CHAMPIONS

THE £1.3 BILLION
DREAM TEAM!

This epic ALL-STAR LINE-UP brings together stars from all over the globe with the biggest price tags in their position!

TRANSFER VALUE
£80M

KEEPER

GIANLUIGI DONNARUMMA

PSG & ITALY

The 23-year-old Italian giant is still a bambino in goalkeeping terms but he's already clocked up almost 300 club games and 50 for his country. Remember his heroics during Italy's Euro 2020 success where he was named Player of the Tournament?

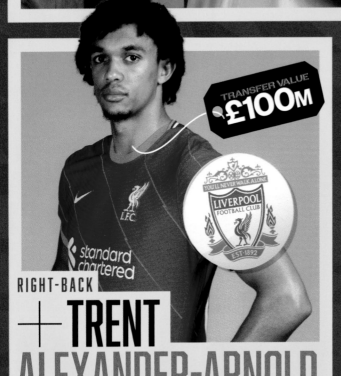

TRANSFER VALUE
£100M

RIGHT-BACK

TRENT ALEXANDER-ARNOLD

LIVERPOOL & ENGLAND

Trent's magical right foot is one of the wonders of the footballing world. He may get filed under R for right-back, but he should really be under P for playmaker. His fizzed 70-yard diagonals and whipped in crosses are a thing of beauty!

TRANSFER VALUE
£90M

CENTRE-BACK

RUBEN DIAS

MAN. CITY & PORTUGAL

What a signing this guy has been for Pep Guardiola. He marshalls the City defence with cool composure and there's very little that gets past him. Oppo forwards will see his name on the team sheet and give a huge groan! He's immense!

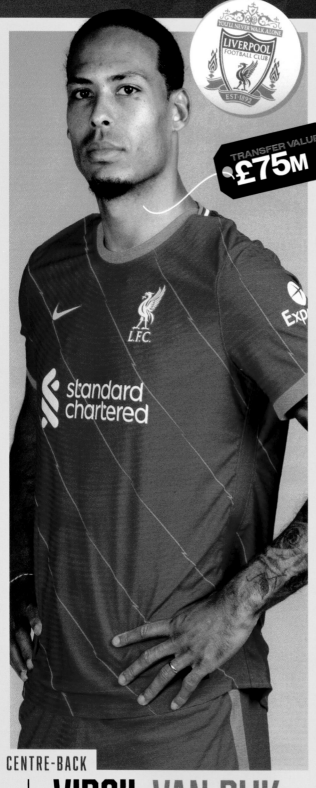

TRANSFER VALUE
£75M

TRANSFER VALUE
£80M

CENTRE-BACK

+VIRGIL VAN DIJK

LIVERPOOL & NETHERLANDS

He may be the wrong side of 30 but Big Virg is still a colossus at the heart of the Reds defence — and still worth a fortune. He's gobbled up a gazillion trophies and awards over the past three years — you're looking at a Prem legend!

LEFT-BACK

+ALPHONSO DAVIES

BAYERN MUNICH & CANADA

We've got Trent's wand of a right foot on the right flank, and the turbo-charged 21-year-old Canadian on the left. The Fonz only made his Bundesliga debut in 2018, but has already won 11 trophies, including four league titles and the UCL!

TRANSFER VALUE
£120M

MIDFIELDER
PHIL FODEN
MAN. CITY & ENGLAND

When Pep Guardiola said: "Phil Foden is the most talented player I have ever seen," the world gasped. But he had a point. The 23-year-old's a legend in the making and even though we've slapped a £120m price tag on him, he's priceless to City!

TRANSFER VALUE
£80M

TRANSFER VALUE
£90M

MIDFIELDER
KEVIN DE BRUYNE
MAN. CITY & BELGIUM

Quite simply, the best, most devastating midfielder in world football. The two-time PFA Player of the Year has led City to no fewer than 11 trophies during his time at the club, and has clocked more than 100 assists. That doesn't come cheap!

MIDFIELDER
PEDRI
BARCELONA & SPAIN

The teenage Spanish baller will be pulling the strings for club and country for the next decade. He's got the tek, the brain and the mentality to become a Nou Camp legend — especially under ex-Barca midfield great Xavi!

TRANSFER VALUE
£120M

TRANSFER VALUE
£220

FORWARD
MOHAMED SALAH
LIVERPOOL & EGYPT

Three Premier League Golden Boot awards, a Prem title, a Champions League title, the FA Cup, the EFL Cup, the FIFA Club World Cup — the Egyptian King has won the lot at Anfield. He's also the PFA Player of the Year, and he guarantees goals!

FORWARD
KYLIAN MBAPPE
PSG & FRANCE

Here he is — the most valuable player in world football. Mbappe, the 23-year-old French goal king, is writing his name into the history books with a big fat marker pen — because he's going to go down as a true great of the game!

TRANSFER VALUE £180M

STRIKER

ERLING HAALAND
MAN. CITY & NORWAY

Thanks to a clause in his Borussia Dortmund contract, City only paid £51m for the 22-year-old goalscoring phenom — but he's worth three times that figure. By the end of the 2021-22 season, he'd scored 114 goals in his last 111 games. Wow!

+ THE MOST EXPENSIVE OF ALL TIME!

Those guys have the biggest price tags right now but what is the most expensive team of all time based on actual transfers that have happened?

KEPA ARRIZABALAGA
ATHLETIC BILBAO TO CHELSEA £72m

JOAO CANCELO
JUVENTUS TO MAN. CITY £60m

HARRY MAGUIRE
LEICESTER TO MAN. UNITED £80m

VIRGIL VAN DIJK
SOUTHAMPTON TO LIVERPOOL £75m

LUCAS HERNANDEZ
A. MADRID TO B. MUNICH £68m

PHILIPPE COUTINHO
LIVERPOOL TO BARCELONA £142m

PAUL POGBA
JUVENTUS TO MAN. UNITED £89m

JACK GREALISH
ASTON VILLA TO MAN. CITY £100m

NEYMAR
BARCELONA TO PSG £198m

JOAO FELIX
BENFICA TO A. MADRID £105m

KYLIAN MBAPPE
MONACO TO PSG £163m

LOOK INTO YOUR FUTURE!

Mystic Moggy has peered into her crystal ball to predict what the Wikipedia profiles may look like for some big-name footy stars once they've retired!

Danny Welbeck

Personal information	
Full name	Daniel Nii Tackie Mensah Welbeck
Date of birth	26 November 1990 (age 31)
Place of birth	Manchester, England
Height	1.85m (6ft 1in)
Playing position	Forward

Senior career

Years	Team	Apps	Goals
2008-14	Man. United	142	29
2010	Preston (loan)	8	2
2010-11	Sunderland (loan)	28	6
2014-19	Arsenal	126	32
2019-20	Watford	20	3
2020-23	Brighton	59	19
2023-24	Juventus	21	17
2024-25	Real Madrid	19	19
2025-26	PSG	9	12
2026-27	Bayern Munich	31	29
2027-28	Man. United	18	1
2028-30	Fylde	33	78
	Total	**514**	**247**

National team

Years	Country	Apps	Goals
2005	England U-16	1	0
2006-07	England U-17	11	2
2007-08	England U-18	2	2
2008-09	England U-19	8	2
2009-11	England U-21	14	5
2011-27	England	45	36

Jude Bellingham

Personal information	
Full name	Jude Victor William Bellingham
Date of birth	29 June 2003 (age 19)
Place of birth	Stourbridge, England
Height	1.86m (6ft 1in)
Playing position	Midfielder

Senior career

Years	Team	Apps	Goals
2019-20	Birmingham	44	4
2020-23	Borussia Dortmund	109	19
2023-33	Liverpool	323	42
2033-34	Everton	17	1
2034-38	Birmingham	119	9
	Total	**612**	**75**

National team

Years	Country	Apps	Goals
2018-19	England U-16	7	4
2019	England U-17	3	2
2020	England U-21	4	1
2020-33	England	101	21

Now create your own Wikipedia profile — and predict your own future!

Raheem Sterling

Personal information

Full name	Raheem Shaquille Sterling
Date of birth	8 December 1994 (age 27)
Place of birth	Kingston, Jamaica
Height	1.70m (5ft 7in)
Playing position	Forward

Senior career

Years	Team	Apps	Goals
2012-15	Liverpool	129	23
2015-22	Man. City	339	131
2022-25	Chelsea	42	19
2025-26	Inter Milan	18	3
2026-28	Atletico Madrid	38	12
2028-30	Benfica	49	11
2030-32	New York City	38	27
	Total	**661**	**236**

National team

Years	Country	Apps	Goals
2009-10	England U-16	7	1
2010-11	England U-17	13	3
2012	England U-19	1	0
2012-13	England U-21	8	3
2012-26	England	97	28

Harry Maguire

Personal information

Full name	Jacob Harry Maguire
Date of birth	5 March 1993 (age 29)
Place of birth	Sheffield, England
Height	1.94m (6ft 4in)
Playing position	Centre-back

Senior career

Years	Team	Apps	Goals
2011-14	Sheffield United	166	12
2014-17	Hull	75	3
2015	Wigan (loan)	16	1
2017-19	Leicester	76	5
2019-24	Man. United	156	9
2024-25	Huddersfield	22	1
2025-27	Rotherham	52	1
2027-30	Bolton	16	2
2028-29	Doncaster (loan)	8	0
2029	Accrington Stanley (loan)	7	1
2029-30	Hearts (loan)	18	1
2030-31	Perth Glory	29	5
2031-32	Halifax	19	2
2032-33	Barrow	6	0
	Total	**661**	**236**

National team

Years	Country	Apps	Goals
2012	England U-21	1	0
2017-24	England	50	9

Stick your photo here

Write your name here

Personal information

Full name	
Date of birth	
Place of birth	
Height	
Playing position	

Senior career

Years	Team	Apps	Goals

National team

Years	Country	Apps	Goals

MY DREAM

+ CLUB FACT FILE! +

Club name ....

Club nickname ....

Stadium name ....

Stadium capacity ....

Club owner [your name] ....

Manager ....

+ THE BADGE! +

ESTD 2022

Design your club's badge!

+ THE KITS! +

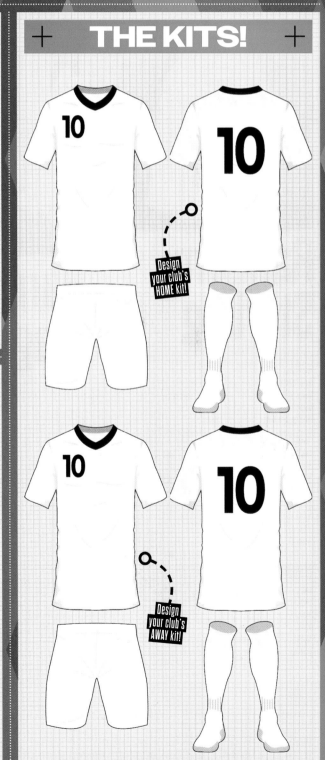

Design your club's HOME kit!

Design your club's AWAY kit!

TEAM FC! +

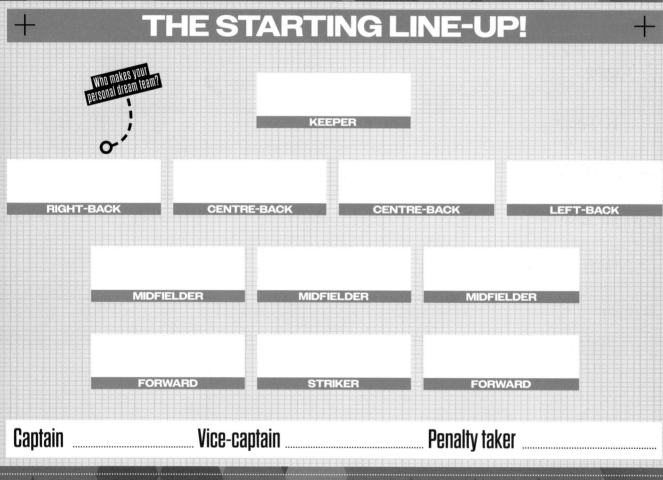

e name, the players, the kit. Absolutely everything!

THE STARTING LINE-UP!

Who makes your personal dream team?

KEEPER

RIGHT-BACK   **CENTRE-BACK**   **CENTRE-BACK**   **LEFT-BACK**

MIDFIELDER   **MIDFIELDER**   **MIDFIELDER**

FORWARD   **STRIKER**   **FORWARD**

Captain .... Vice-captain .... Penalty taker ....

THE BOOTS!

Design your star player's footy boot!

THE PLAYING STYLE!

- ☑ Attacking
- ☑ Defensive
- ☑ Passing
- ☑ Direct
- ☑ Counter-attack
- ☑ High tempo
- ☑ Long ball
- ☑ Patient

THE ALTERNATIVE WORLD CUPS OF FOOTBALL!

This is your chance to decide – once and for all – just what are
THE BEST THINGS in this big incredible world of football!

WHAT YOU NEED TO DO!

◼ We've drawn each first round at random — the rest is up to you!

◼ Decide who wins each match-up, the winner goes through to the next round and sets up another match-up!

◼ Continue until you have **ONE** team left — this is officially the winner!

THE WORLD CUP OF
HALF-TIME FOOD!

What is the best grub you can get at a match?

MEAT PIE
CRISPS
TWIX
CORNISH PASTY
BURGER
VEGGIE PIE
FRUIT PASTILLES
CHIPS

HOTDOG
HARIBO
SAUSAGE ROLL
MALTESERS
PIZZA
MARS BAR
SKITTLES
BACON ROLL

WINNER!

THE WORLD CUP OF
FOOTY GOATS!

Who is the greatest footballer of all time? You decide!

CRISTIANO RONALDO
FRANZ BECKENBAUER
JOHAN CRUYFF
PELE

ZINEDINE ZIDANE
DIEGO MARADONA
GEORGE BEST
LIONEL MESSI

WINNER!

KEEPERS!

Who is the best keeper in the world? You decide!

JAN OBLAK

HUGO LLORIS

MANUEL NEUER

AARON RAMSDALE

UNAI SIMON

EDERSON

ALISSON BECKER

MARC-ANDRÉ TER STEGEN

JOSE SA

EDOUARD MENDY

DAVID DE GEA

THIBAUT COURTOIS

GIANLUIGI DONNARUMMA

JORDAN PICKFORD

EMILIANO MARTINEZ

KASPER SCHMEICHEL

WINNER!

THE WORLD CUP OF

SUPERCLUBS!

Which is the biggest club in the world? You decide!

INTER MILAN

LIVERPOOL

BARCELONA

JUVENTUS

CHELSEA

BORUSSIA DORTMUND

REAL MADRID

AC MILAN

ATLETICO MADRID

MAN. UNITED

MAN. CITY

AJAX

BAYERN MUNICH

ARSENAL

PSG

TOTTENHAM

WINNER!

THE WORLD CUP OF
WOMEN BALLERS!

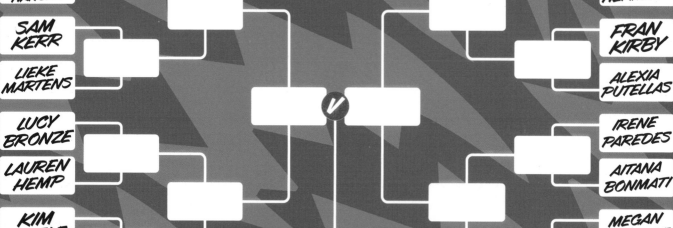

Who is the best female footy star in the world? You decide!

PERNILLE HARDER

CAROLINE GRAHAM HANSEN

SAM KERR

LIEKE MARTENS

LUCY BRONZE

LAUREN HEMP

KIM LITTLE

ALEXANDRA POPP

VIVIANNE MIEDEMA

JENNI HERMOSO

FRAN KIRBY

ALEXIA PUTELLAS

IRENE PAREDES

AITANA BONMATI

MEGAN RAPINOE

ADA HEGERBERG

WINNER!

THE WORLD CUP OF
FOOTY MANAGERS!

Who is the best manager in the world? You decide!

PEP GUARDIOLA

HANSI FLICK

JURGEN KLOPP

JULEN LOPETEGUI

LUIS ENRIQUE

ANTONIO CONTE

CARLO ANCELOTTI

JULIAN NAGELSMANN

DIEGO SIMEONE

ROBERTO MANCINI

THOMAS TUCHEL

DIDIER DESCHAMPS

MAURICIO POCHETTINO

ERIK TEN HAG

XAVI

GARETH SOUTHGATE

WINNER!

Who's won what over the past decade? Here you go...

	2012-13	2013-14	2014-15
PREMIER LEAGUE	Man. United	Man. City	Chelsea
GOLDEN BOOT	 Robin van Persie Man. United	 Luis Suarez Liverpool	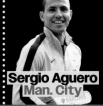 Sergio Aguero Man. City
FA CUP	Wigan	Arsenal	Arsenal
EFL CUP	Swansea	Man. City	Chelsea
PFA PLAYER OF THE YEAR	 Gareth Bale Tottenham	 Luis Suarez Liverpool	 Eden Hazard Chelsea
PFA YOUNG PLAYER OF THE YEAR	  Gareth Bale Tottenham	 Eden Hazard Chelsea	 Harry Kane Tottenham

2015-16	2016-17	2017-18	2018-19	2019-20	2020-21	2021-22
Leicester	Chelsea	Man. City	Man. City	Liverpool	Man. City	Man. City
Harry Kane **Tottenham**	Harry Kane **Tottenham**	Mohamed Salah **Liverpool**	P.E. Aubameyang, Sadio Mane & Mohamed Salah	Jamie Vardy **Leicester**	Harry Kane **Tottenham**	Son Heung-Min & Mohamed Salah
Man. United	Arsenal	Chelsea	Man. City	Arsenal	Leicester	Liverpool
Man. City	Man. United	Man. City	Man. City	Man. City	Man. City	Liverpool
Riyad Mahrez **Leicester**	N'Golo Kante **Chelsea**	Mohamed Salah **Liverpool**	Virgil van Dijk **Liverpool**	Kevin De Bruyne **Man. City**	Kevin De Bruyne **Man. City**	Mohamed Salah **Liverpool**
Dele Alli **Tottenham**	Dele Alli **Tottenham**	Leroy Sane **Man. City**	Raheem Sterling **Man. City**	Trent Alexander -Arnold **Liverpool**	Phil Foden **Man. City**	Phil Foden **Man. City**

65

10 YEARS IN FOOTBALL!

And here's who's grabbed all the silverware in Europe!

	2012-13	2013-14	2014-15
LA LIGA	Barcelona	A. Madrid	Barcelona
BUNDESLIGA	Bayern Munich	 Bayern Munich	Bayern Munich
SERIE A	 Juventus	 Juventus	 Juventus
LIGUE 1	PSG	 PSG	 PSG
CHAMPIONS LEAGUE	 Bayern Munich	 Real Madrid	 Barcelona
EUROPA LEAGUE	Chelsea	 Sevilla	 Sevilla

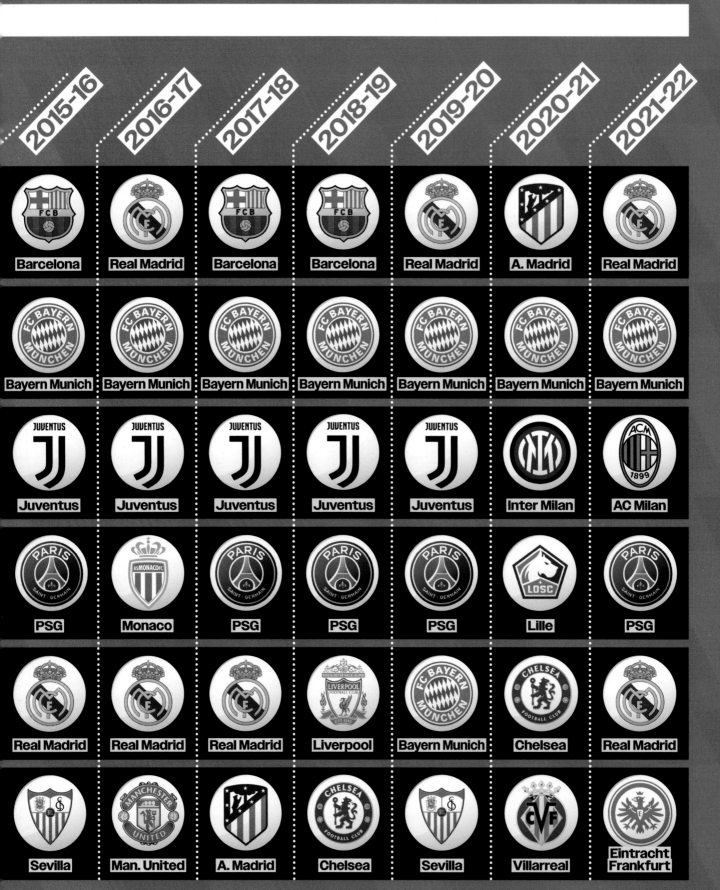

	2015-16	2016-17	2017-18	2018-19	2019-20	2020-21	2021-22
	Barcelona	Real Madrid	Barcelona	Barcelona	Real Madrid	A. Madrid	Real Madrid
	Bayern Munich	Bayern Munich	Bayern Munich	Bayern Munich	Bayern Munich	Bayern Munich	Bayern Munich
	Juventus	Juventus	Juventus	Juventus	Juventus	Inter Milan	AC Milan
	PSG	Monaco	PSG	PSG	PSG	Lille	PSG
	Real Madrid	Real Madrid	Real Madrid	Liverpool	Bayern Munich	Chelsea	Real Madrid
	Sevilla	Man. United	A. Madrid	Chelsea	Sevilla	Villarreal	Eintracht Frankfurt

KEVIN DE BRUYNE

BELGIUM

MIDFIELDER

2022 WORLD CUP ICON!

A YEAR IN FOOTBALL!

How much can you remember about what WENT DOWN IN 2022? Let's find out!

1
Who was named PFA Player of the Year last season?
A KEVIN DE BRUYNE
B MOHAMED SALAH
C HARRY KANE

2
What was the score in the 2021-22 FA Cup final?
A CHELSEA 0-0 LIVERPOOL
B CHELSEA 1-1 LIVERPOOL
C CHELSEA 2-2 LIVERPOOL

3
Which Chelsea player made the 2021-22 PFA TOTY?
A MASON MOUNT
B ANTONIO RUDIGER
C EDOUARD MENDY

4
Who finished bottom of the Prem last season?
A BURNLEY
B NORWICH
C WATFORD

5
Who was sacked as Everton boss back in January?
A CARLO ANCELOTTI
B RAFA BENITEZ
C NUNO ESPIRITO SANTO

6
Which WSL club won the league and FA Cup last season?
A ARSENAL
B CHELSEA
C MAN. CITY

7
Who beat Rangers in the final of the Europa League?
A RB LEIPZIG
B REAL BETIS
C EINTRACHT FRANKFURT

8
Who scored the winner in the 2022 UCL final?
A KARIM BENZEMA
B VINICIUS JUNIOR
C LUKA MODRIC

9
Who finished top scorer in Serie A last season?
A CIRO IMMOBILE
B DUSAN VLAHOVIC
C TAMMY ABRAHAM

YOUR FOOTY BRAIN POWER

YOUR SCORE [ ]/9

9	GENIUS
7	PROFESSIONAL
5	SEMI-PRO
3	AMATEUR
1	SUNDAY LEAGUE
0	OH NO, DISASTER

ANSWERS ON P92

MATCH OF THE DAY MAGAZINE

ROBERT LEWANDOWSKI

POLAND STRIKER

2022 WORLD CUP ICON!

THE WORLD'S TOUGHEST FOOTY QUIZ!

Seriously, readers – this one is going to really stump you!

ANSWERS ON P92

1

Lukasz Fabianski is...

A A large flightless bird found roaming the African savanna

B A type of corn kernel which expands and puffs up when heated

C A footballer who plays as a keeper for West Ham and Poland

2

James Milner is...

A A savoury snack consisting of sausage meat wrapped in puffed pastry

B A yellow sea sponge who lives in a pineapple house

C A veteran footballer who plays as a midfielder for Liverpool

3

Fred is...

A A short Pokemon covered in yellow fur with electrical abilities

B A four-legged, armoured dinosaur from the Jurassic period

C A footballer who plays as a midfielder for Man. United and Brazil

4

Antonio Conte is...

A A Wookiee warrior and Han Solo's Millennium Falcon co-pilot

B A mammal with black velvety fur, poor eyesight and large claws

C A former Italian footballer, now the manager of Tottenham

5

Goodison Park is...

A A strip of facial hair grown above the upper lip

B A fictional British boarding school of magic for students aged 11 to 18

C A football stadium in Liverpool, and the home of Everton

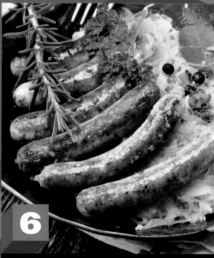

6

Conor Coady is...

A A German sausage made from veal, beef or most commonly pork

B A ferocious fish that inhabits South American rivers and lakes

C A footballer who plays as a centre-back for Wolves and England

TOP 10

BIGGEST CLUB STADIUMS IN EUROPE!

NOU CAMP 99,354
LOCATION Barcelona, Spain
BUILT 1957 HOME OF Barcelona

1

WESTFALENSTADION 81,359
LOCATION Dortmund, Germany
BUILT 1974 HOME OF Borussia Dortmund

2

SANTIAGO BERNABEU 81,044
LOCATION Madrid, Spain
BUILT 1947 HOME OF Real Madrid

3

SAN SIRO 78,275
LOCATION Milan, Italy
BUILT 1926 HOME OF AC Milan & Inter Milan

4

ATATURK OLYMPIC STADIUM 75,145
LOCATION Istanbul, Turkey
BUILT 2002 HOME OF Fatih Karagumruk

5

OLYMPIC STADIUM 75,000
LOCATION Athens, Greece
BUILT 1982 HOME OF AEK Athens

6=

ALLIANZ ARENA 75,000
LOCATION Munich, Germany
BUILT 2005 HOME OF Bayern Munich

6=

OLD TRAFFORD 74,879
LOCATION Manchester, England
BUILT 1910 HOME OF Man. United

8

OLYMPIASTADION 74,649
LOCATION Berlin, Germany
BUILT 1936 HOME OF Hertha Berlin

9

STADIO OLIMPICO 70,634
LOCATION Rome, Italy
BUILT 1930 HOME OF Roma & Lazio

10

PEDRI

SPAIN

MIDFIELDER

2022 WORLD CUP
ICON!

BEARD *RANKINGS!*

We rank the MOST ICONIC BEARDS in the history of football – from the best to the worst!

ELITE TIER

MARCO SAILER

DAVIDE MOSCARDELLI

WORLD CLASS TIER

ANDREA PIRLO

RAUL MEIRELES

MILE JEDINAK

JIMMY DURMAZ

JO INGE BERGET

PROFESSIONAL TIER

ROY KEANE

JOE LEDLEY

MARC CROSAS

BORJA VALERO

MICHAEL BOSTWICK

SEMI-PROFESSIONAL TIER

STUART SINCLAIR

PAUL BREITNER

SANDRO

SCOTT WAGSTAFF

BRIAN LITTLE

AMATEUR TIER

ANDY CARROLL

ALEXI LALAS

ALESSANDRO MELLI

DAVID DE GEA

ABEL XAVIER

2022 WORLD CUP
ICON!

SADIO

MANE

SENEGAL
FORWARD

MATCH
OF THE
DAY
MAGAZINE

THE ULTIMATE FOOTY QUIZ!

Good luck!

YOUR MISSION

■ To complete ALL difficulty levels and prove you are a 100% footy genius!

THE RULES

■ Start with level 1 BEGINNER, then work your way through the questions!

■ Once you've mastered each level, move on to the next for a more challenging experience!

■ You are officially a footy genius if you can complete all four levels, including the formidable WORLD-CLASS level!

LOADING LEVEL 1...

2 POINTS FOR EACH CORRECT ANSWER!

1 NAME THE PLAYER!

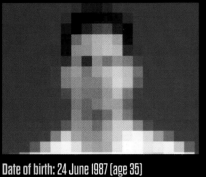

Date of birth: 24 June 1987 (age 35)
Born: Rosario, Argentina Position: Forward

YEARS	TEAM	GAMES/GOALS
2004-21	Barcelona	778/672
2021-	PSG	28/8
2005-	Argentina	160/81

2 NAME THE TEAM!

PEACE — МИР   PEACE

3 NAME THE LEGEND!

4 NAME THE CLUB!

Founded: 1878 Country: England Stadium:
Goodison Park (39,414) Nickname: The Toffees

ANSWERS ON P92

5 NAME THE COUNTRY!

Where would you find these clubs?

DIFFICULTY LEVEL BEGINNER MY SCORE ☐ /10

LOADING LEVEL 2...

2 POINTS FOR EACH CORRECT ANSWER!

1 NAME THE PLAYER!

Date of birth: 9 September 1985 (age 36)
Born: Zadar, Croatia Position: Midfielder

YEARS	TEAM	GAMES/GOALS
2003-08	Dinamo Zagreb	128/32
2003-04	Zrinjski Mostar (loan)	25/8
2004-05	Inter Zaprešić (loan)	18/4
2008-12	Tottenham	159/17
2012-	Real Madrid	428/31
2006-	Croatia	148/21

2 NAME THE TEAM!

3 NAME THE LEGEND!

4 NAME THE CLUB!

Founded: 1882 Country: England Stadium:
Turf Moor (21,944) Nickname: The Clarets

ANSWERS ON P92

5 NAME THE COUNTRY!

Where would you find these clubs?

DIFFICULTY LEVEL **AMATEUR** MY SCORE ☐ /10

LOADING LEVEL 3...

2 POINTS FOR EACH CORRECT ANSWER!

1 NAME THE PLAYER!

Date of birth: 11 January 1996 (age 26)
Born: Essen, Germany **Position:** Winger

YEARS	TEAM	GAMES/GOALS
2014-16	Schalke	57/13
2016-20	Man. City	135/39
2020-	Bayern Munich	85/24
2015-	Germany	42/11

....

2 NAME THE TEAM!

....

3 NAME THE LEGEND!

....

4 NAME THE CLUB!

Founded: 1903 **Country:** Scotland **Stadium:**
Pittodrie Stadium (20,866) **Nickname:** The Dons

....

ANSWERS ON P92

5 NAME THE COUNTRY!

Where would you find these clubs?

....

DIFFICULTY LEVEL PROFESSIONAL MY SCORE ☐

LOADING LEVEL 4...

2 POINTS FOR EACH CORRECT ANSWER!

1 NAME THE PLAYER!

Date of birth: 24 September 1991 (age 30)
Born: Ulldecona. Spain Position: Midfielder

YEARS	TEAM	GAMES/GOALS
2010-11	Barcelona	2/0
2011-15	Chelsea	9/1
2013-14	Valencia (loan)	8/0
2014-15	Stuttgart (loan)	28/0
2015-	Southampton	247/7

2 NAME THE TEAM!

3 NAME THE LEGEND!

4 NAME THE CLUB!

Founded: 1950 Country: England Stadium:
Pirelli Stadium (6.912) Nickname: The Brewers

ANSWERS ON P92

5 NAME THE COUNTRY!
Where would you find these clubs?

DIFFICULTY LEVEL WORLD CLASS MY SCORE ☐ **GAME OVER**

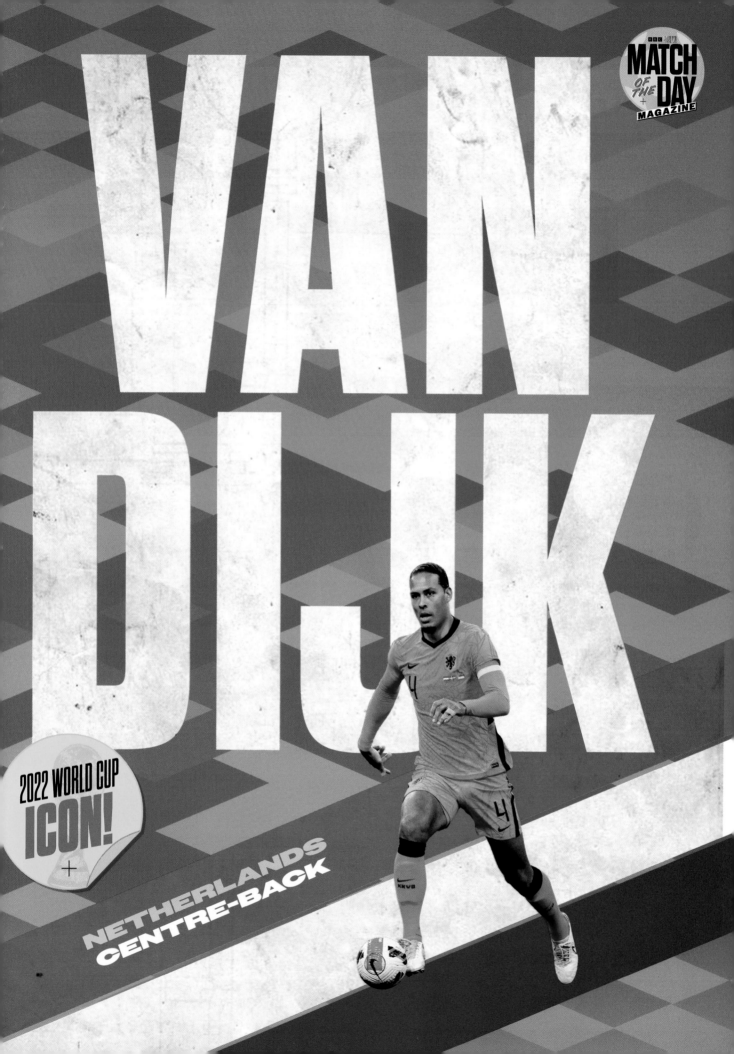

VAN DIJK

MATCH OF THE DAY MAGAZINE

2022 WORLD CUP ICON!

**NETHERLANDS
CENTRE-BACK**

WHO ARE YA?

ANSWERS ON *P92*

UNDER-16 CONTENDER NAME ....

All these players played in the Premier League during the 2021-22 SEASON – can you name them?

1

A OLLIE WATKINS
B JACOB RAMSEY
C EZRI KONSA

2

A SHANE DUFFY
B LEWIS DUNK
C ADAM WEBSTER

3

A FABIO SILVA
B RUBEN NEVES
C JOAO MOUTINHO

4

A LUKE AYLING
B STUART DALLAS
C JACK HARRISON

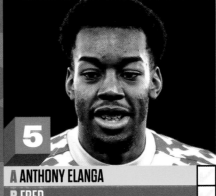

5

A ANTHONY ELANGA
B FRED
C AARON WAN-BISSAKA

6

A KIERNAN DEWSBURY-HALL
B LUKE THOMAS
C HARVEY BARNES

7

A JOEL MATIP
B THIAGO ALCANTARA
C FABINHO

8

A RODRI
B JOAO CANCELO
C RUBEN DIAS

U16 SCORE ☐ /9

9

A MARC GUEHI
B EBERECHI EZE
C MICHAEL OLISE

KIDS V GROWN UPS!

ADULT CONTENDER NAME ....

All these players played in the Premier League during the 2001-02 SEASON – can you name them?

1

- **A** IAN HARTE
- **B** STEVE FINNAN
- **C** STEPHEN CARR

2

- **A** DARREN BENT
- **B** TITUS BRAMBLE
- **C** MARCUS BENT

3

- **A** JESPER GRONKJAER
- **B** BOUDEWIJN ZENDEN
- **C** GABRIELE AMBROSETTI

4

- **A** DAVID BELLION
- **B** QUINTON FORTUNE
- **C** ERIC DJEMBA-DJEMBA

5
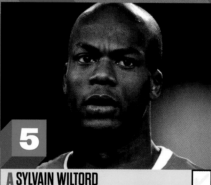
- **A** SYLVAIN WILTORD
- **B** CHRISTOPHER WREH
- **C** LUIS BOA MORTE

6

- **A** LAUREN
- **B** GEREMI
- **C** RIGOBERT SONG

7

- **A** STEFAN IVERSEN
- **B** CHRISTIAN ZIEGE
- **C** NICK BARMBY

8

- **A** BOSKO BALABAN
- **B** SAVO MILOSEVIC
- **C** JUAN PABLO ANGEL

ADULT SCORE ☐ /9

9
- **A** ROBBIE EARLE
- **B** DARRYL POWELL
- **C** CHRIS POWELL

85

THE A-Z OF THE WORLD'S BEST WOMEN BALLERS!

FACT FILE Full name: Kosovare Asllani Age: 33 Club: AC Milan Country: Sweden Position: Forward

A IS FOR ASLLANI

Let's start with A, and AC Milan's new striker. This Swedish goal-getter, who's played more than 160 games for her country and lists PSG, Man. City and Real Madrid as former clubs, joined the Italians in June!

FACT FILE Full name: Christiane Endler Age: 31 Club: Lyon Country: Chile Position: Keeper

E IS FOR ENDLER

Say hello to the best keeper in the world. The South American, who won the French league with PSG last year, is a commanding presence between the posts — and she helped new club Lyon win the Champions League back in May!

FACT FILE Full name: Aitana Bonmati **Age:** 24
Club: Barcelona **Country:** Spain **Position:** Midfielder

B IS FOR BONMATI

Aitana is the first of a bajillion Barcelona ballers in our list. The skilful midfielder, who came through Barca's famous academy, is now a key player for club and country — regularly assisting and scoring on the biggest stages!

FACT FILE Full name: Mariona Caldentey **Age:** 26
Club: Barcelona **Country:** Spain **Position:** Forward

C IS FOR CALDENTEY

Another Spaniard and another Barca star, but Mariona didn't come through the club's youth system. The tricky forward grew up on the island of Majorca and could yet be the Balearics' best sporting export since Rafa Nadal!

FACT FILE Full name: Kadidiatou Diani **Age:** 27
Club: PSG **Country:** France **Position:** Forward

D IS FOR DIANI

Defenders see this French flyer in their sleep — because she's a nightmare to play against. She's quick, direct and skips past full-backs as if they're not there. She has also hit 51 goals in her last 75 games for PSG!

FACT FILE Full name: Geyse Ferreira **Age:** 24 **Club:** Barcelona **Country:** Brazil **Position:** Forward

F IS FOR FERREIRA

This explosive Brazilian striker was joint-top scorer in Spain's Primera Division last season — and it was that red-hot form which saw her leave Madrid CFF this summer to seal a dream move to Barcelona!

FACT FILE Full name: Cristiana Girelli **Age:** 32
Club: Juventus **Country:** Italy **Position:** Striker

G IS FOR GIRELLI

Most Italians be hungry for a bowl of penne arrabbiata or a classic margherita drizzled with olive oil, but not Cristiana — she's just hungry for goals. The Juve striker has netted almost 300 for club and country!

FACT FILE Full name: Caroline Graham Hansen **Age:** 27
Club: Barcelona **Country:** Norway **Position:** Midfielder

H IS FOR HANSEN

H was a tough choice for this list. You've got Pernille Harder at Chelsea, Lyon's Ada Hegerberg and Jennifer Hermoso of Barcelona — but we've gone for her silky-skilled team-mate, Caroline Graham Hansen!

FACT FILE Full name: Mana Iwabuchi Age: 29 Club: Arsenal Country: Japan Position: Midfielder

I IS FOR IWABUCHI

Mana is one of the game's most technically gifted ballers, with an immaculate touch, an eye for a pass and unbelievable close control. She made her international debut at 16 and is now the face of Japanese football!

FACT FILE Full name: Ji So-Yun Age: 31 Club: Suwon Country: South Korea Position: Midfielder

J IS FOR JI

South Korea's all-time top goalscorer, who spent eight years with Chelsea, is arguably the best foreign player in the history of the WSL. The classy play-maker returned home to Suwon, in South Korea, in the summer!

FACT FILE Full name: Sam Kerr Age: 28 Club: Chelsea Country: Australia Position: Striker

K IS FOR KERR

The world's deadliest striker is the only player to have won the Golden Boot in three different leagues — Australia, USA and England, where she's won it the last two years. Her finishing is incisive, her numbers insane — she's incredible!

FACT FILE Full name: Kim Little **Age:** 32 **Club:** Arsenal **Country:** Scotland **Position:** Midfielder

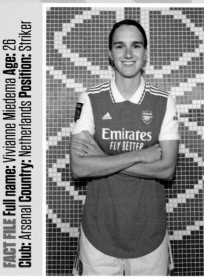

FACT FILE Full name: Vivianne Miedema **Age:** 26 **Club:** Arsenal **Country:** Netherlands **Position:** Striker

FACT FILE Full name: Alyssa Naeher **Age:** 34 **Club:** Chicago Red Stars **Country:** USA **Position:** Keeper

L IS FOR LITTLE

Huge shouts to PSG full-back Ashley Lawrence, Lyon forward Eugenie Le Sommer and Barcelona defender Mapi Leon — but we've plumped for this goalscoring midfielder and Scotland's best-ever player as our L star!

M IS FOR MIEDEMA

M is another letter with a ton of top-quality ballers — we're looking at you Lieke Martens, you Sam Mewis and you Dzsenifer Marozsan. But we can't pick anyone other than the WSL's all-time top scorer — Viv is a total goal-machine!

N IS FOR NAEHER

The second keeper in our list is the USA's No.1, who has racked up more than 80 caps for her country over the past nine years — and played a massive role when the USWNT won the Women's World Cup back in 2019!

FACT FILE Full name: Asisat Oshoala **Age:** 27 **Club:** Barcelona **Country:** Nigeria **Position:** Forward

FACT FILE Full name: Alexia Putellas **Age:** 28 **Club:** Barcelona **Country:** Spain **Position:** Midfielder

FACT FILE Full name: Quinn **Age:** 26 **Club:** OL Reign **Country:** Canada **Position:** Midfielder

O IS FOR OSHOALA

The ex-Liverpool and Arsenal forward is now part of the women's game's most fearsome attack. She was the Spanish league's joint-top scorer last season, which took her Barcelona tally to an incredible 58 goals in just 64 games!

P IS FOR PUTELLAS

Spain's most-capped player of all time has got the lot — she scores (36 goals in the last two seasons), she assists, she dictates play — she was the world's best female player before getting injured in July!

Q IS FOR QUINN

The Canadian midfielder, who's won 68 caps for their country, won a gold medal at the 2020 Tokyo Olympics — and in doing so, also became the first openly non-binary transgender athlete to compete at an Olympic Games!

FACT FILE **Full name:** Christine Sinclair **Age:** 39 **Club:** Portland Thorns **Country:** Canada **Position:** Midfielder

S IS FOR SINCLAIR

Just like Renard, this Canadian icon is a genuine legend of the game. She's played a mind-boggling 310 times for her country, has scored an equally crazy 189 goals, and last summer led them to gold at the Tokyo Olympics!

FACT FILE **Full name:** Wendie Renard **Age:** 32 **Club:** Lyon **Country:** France **Position:** Centre-back

R IS FOR RENARD

Renard is a true one-club wonder. The French star has played over 400 games for Lyon over 16 seasons, winning 14 French league titles, eight Champions League titles and scoring more than 130 goals from centre-back. Wow!

FACT FILE **Full name:** Marta Torrejón **Age:** 32 **Club:** Barcelona **Country:** Spain **Position:** Defender

T IS FOR TORREJON

The seventh Barcelona star in our A-Z, but the first defender. Torrejon has won 18 trophies in the last 17 years — including six Spanish league titles and the Champions League — and won 90 caps for Spain before retiring in 2019!

FACT FILE Full name: Catalina Usme **Age:** 32 **Club:** America De Cali **Country:** Colombia **Position:** Forward

FACT FILE Full name: Danielle van de Donk **Age:** 31 **Club:** Lyon **Country:** Netherlands **Position:** Midfielder

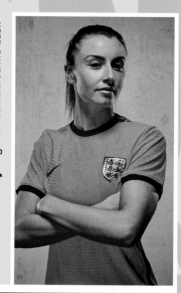

FACT FILE Full name: Leah Williamson **Age:** 25 **Club:** Arsenal **Country:** England **Position:** Centre-back

U IS FOR USME

One of South America's most gifted forwards — and her country's all-time top scorer — is a predator in front of goal. She was top scorer in the Colombian league last season as she fired America De Cali to the title!

V IS FOR VAN DE DONK

The Donk, who's won almost 130 caps for the Netherlands, has been one of the game's heroes over the past decade — starring in her homeland, in Sweden and for Arsenal in the WSL. Now she's doing the business in France for Lyon!

W IS FOR WILLIAMSON

England captain Leah is the ultimate baller, whether she's playing in defence or midfield. She's calm and composed, and can ping 60-yard passes for fun. No wonder she's clocked up more than 200 games for club and country!

FACT FILE Full name: Riola Xhemaili **Age:** 19 **Club:** Freiburg **Country:** Switzerland **Position:** Midfielder

FACT FILE Full name: Tameka Yallop **Age:** 31 **Club:** West Ham **Country:** Australia **Position:** Midfielder

FACT FILE Full name: Manuela Zinsberger **Age:** 26 **Club:** Arsenal **Country:** Austria **Position:** Keeper

X IS FOR XHEMAILI

Let's be honest, there aren't many names out there that begin with X. But this teenage Swiss midfielder is highly rated. She helped her club to mid-table in the German league and she already has 13 caps for her country!

Y IS FOR YALLOP

West Ham's midfielder, who's played more than 100 times for Australia, has clocked up serious air-miles in a career which has seen her play in the USA, Japan, Sweden, Norway, her homeland and now, of course, England!

Z IS FOR ZINSBERGER

The Gunners' keeper is firmly established as one of the best in the WSL — keeping more clean sheets last season than anyone else. She's won the league in Austria, in Germany and now dreams of doing it in England!

ANSWERS!

How did you get on with all our EPIC QUIZZES? It's time to find out!

THE CHAMPIONS QUIZ!

FROM P9

1 A, 2 C, 3 B, 4 C, 5 C,
6 B, 7 A, 8 A, 9 B

A YEAR IN FOOTBALL!

FROM P69

1 B, 2 A, 3 B, 4 B, 5 B,
6 B, 7 C, 8 B, 9 A

WORLD'S TOUGHEST FOOTY QUIZ!
FROM P71

1 C, 2 C, 3 C,
4 C, 5 C, 6 C

ULTIMATE FOOTY QUIZ

FROM P77!

BEGINNER 1 LIONEL MESSI,
2 REAL MADRID, 3 THIERRY HENRY,
4 EVERTON, 5 ITALY

AMATEUR 1 LUKA MODRIC,
2 AC MILAN, 3 DIDIER DROGBA,
4 BURNLEY, 5 FRANCE

PROFESSIONAL 1 LEROY SANE,
2 ROMA, 3 ROBBIE FOWLER,
4 ABERDEEN, 5 PORTUGAL

WORLD CLASS 1 ORIOL ROMEU,
2 RANGERS, 3 JUNINHO,
4 BURTON, 5 BELGIUM

WHO ARE YA?

FROM P84-85

UNDER-16 CONTENDER
1 C, 2 A, 3 B,
4 B, 5 A, 6 C,
7 A, 8 B, 9 C

ADULT CONTENDER
1 B, 2 C, 3 A,
4 B, 5 A, 6 C,
7 B, 8 A, 9 C

MATCH OF THE DAY MAGAZINE

BBC

THE UK'S BEST-SELLING FOOTY MAG!

OUT EVERY FORTNIGHT!

MATCH OF THE DAY MAGAZINE

Write to us at *Match of the Day magazine,
Immediate Media, Vineyard House,
44 Brook Green, Hammersmith, London, W6 7BT*
Telephone **020 7150 5513** Email *inbox@motdmag.com*

Match of the Day mag editor	**Mark Parry**
Head of content	**Lee Stobbs**
Senior art editor	**Blue Buxton**
Senior designer	**Bradley Wooldridge**
Annual designer	**Pete Rogers**
Senior writer / digital creator	**Jake Wilson**

Group picture editor	**Natasha Thompson**
Picture editor	**Jason Timson**
Production editor	**Neil Queen-Jones**
Sub-editor	**Johnny Sharp**
Editorial director	**Corinna Shaffer**
Annual images	**Getty Images**

BBC Books an imprint of Ebury Publishing 20 Vauxhall Bridge Road London SW1V 2SA. BBC Books is part of the Penguin Random House group of companies whose addresses can be found at global. penguinrandomhouse.com. Copyright © Match Of The Day magazine 2022. First published by BBC Books in 2022 www.penguin.co.uk. A CIP catalogue record for this book is available from the British Library. ISBN 9781785946806. Commissioning editor: Albert DePetrillo; project editor: Iman Khabca; editorial assistant: Céline Nyssens; production: Phil Spencer. Printed and bound in Italy by Elcograf S.p.A. The authorised representative in the EEA is Penguin Random House Ireland, Morrison Chambers, 32 Nassau Street, Dublin D02 YH68 Penguin Random House is committed to a sustainable future for our business our readers and our planet. This book is made from Forest Stewardship Council ® certified paper.

FAKE

FOOTBALL NEWS

Home | Premier League | **Football League** | European | Women's | Transfers | Badgers |

Bruce's moose on the loose

Panicked shoppers fled for safety in West Bromwich this afternoon as Steve Bruce's pet moose escaped – causing chaos in the town's main shopping centre for six hours.

The animal, who lodges in Bruce's spare room, was eventually wrestled to the ground by ex-England boss Sam Allardyce, who was out picking up his weekly supply of sausage rolls.

Startled pensioner Bert McSquirt, 82, said: "At first I thought it were a goose – but, oh no, it were a moose."

🕐 18 mins | Midlands | 💬 324

▶ **Debate: Is a moose actually an elk?**
▶ **Six delicious chocolate mousse recipes**
▶ **Q&A: how to catch a moose with only a packet of Quavers**

Benteke stars v Mars

Earth will take a slender 1-0 lead to Mars for the second leg of their Intergalactic Cup semi-final after a bad-tempered clash against The Martians. Christian Benteke's second-half header separated the two teams in a match which saw the visitors reduced to eight players following a mass on-pitch brawl. Despite the win, Earth boss Neil Warnock was in no mood to celebrate: "I hate those aliens," he ranted.

🕐 3h | North west |